Praise for
THE BLUEFISH COOKBOOK

"Excellent recipes. Splendid instructions." —**The New York Times**

"Charming...obviously a labor of love." —**Bon Appetit**

"The most complete collection of bluefish recipes around, ranging from simple to elaborate to the somewhat wacky."
—**The Boston Globe**

"A truly superior little cookbook" —**The Martha's Vineyard Times**

"Each year bluefish explode along the eastern seaboard...soon everyone is up to his boots in bluefish. The first few taste wonderful. The second taste almost as good...but pretty soon the bluefish blahs begin to set in. To the rescue come the authors of *The Bluefish Cookbook* with recipes ranging from Bluefish Hash, Bluefish with Gin, to salads, cakes and chowders...This is a book with salt breezes blowing through the pages—a fine cookbook done by two who know their blues." —**Seafood Leader**

THE Bluefish COOKBOOK

FOURTH EDITION, REVISED AND EXPANDED
INCLUDES NEW LOW-CALORIE
RECIPES

Greta Jacobs & Jane Alexander

Illustrated by Wezi Swift

The Globe Pequot Press

Chester, Connecticut

About the Authors

Besides being a fine cook, Jane Alexander is an accomplished actress of both film and theater. She has been nominated for four Academy awards. She won a Tony for her role in *The Great White Hope* and an Emmy for *Playing Time*, and she starred as Eleanor Roosevelt in the award winning *Eleanor and Franklin*. She is married to the director Ed Sherin and is the mother of four boys. Her other interests include bird watching and photography.

Greta Jacobs, mother of nine children and grandmother of thirteen, has much experience as a gourmet cook. She enjoys gardening, skiing, birding, and volunteer work. A worldwide traveler, she also enjoys a house on Bantry Bay in Ireland. A longtime resident of Nantucket, she now resides in Old Saybrook, Connecticut.

Library of Congress Cataloging-in-Publication data

Jacobs, Greta
    The bluefish cookbook / Greta Jacobs and Jane Alexander :
    illustrated by Wezi Swift. — 4th ed., rev. and expanded
       p.   cm.
    ISBN 0-87106-467-7
    1. Cookery (bluefish)   I. Alexander, Jane.   II. Title.
    TX748.B55J33 1990
    641.6'92 — dc20   89-77345
                                  CIP

Manufactured in the United States of America
Fourth Edition/First Printing

We contemplated calling this book "What to do when you've got the Blues." Because when the bluefish are running off the Atlantic coast and there are fisherpersons among your family or friends, bluefish can become a staple of your daily diet. The fillets are delicious simply baked with salt and pepper and dotted with butter. Knowing how wonderfully special this fine fish tastes, after years of preparing them a variety of ways, we thought we'd share some of our experience. We are grateful to our friends for including some of their favorite recipes too.

Most of the recipes call for the fillets of the fish, which we feel are superior to the whole fish in cooking. If you do not know how to fillet, we suggest you ask someone who does.

Do not wash the fillets before cooking; to preserve flavor pat them dry with paper towels.

Because bluefish usually weigh between two and fifteen pounds, the number of portions you can serve will depend on the size of your fish. The fillets from a six-pound fish will serve four generously. Accordingly, the recipes in this book will serve four, unless indicated otherwise.

A good rule of thumb for cooking time is ten minutes per inch thickness of fish at its thickest part, or until the fish is just cooked through, and no more.

And, lastly, to aid in your cleanup, bake the fish on a sheet of foil if you are using a metal pan.

Bon Appétit

Greta Jacobs
Jane Alexander

NANTUCKET

This symbol, found on some of our recipes, represents recipes lower in fat and/or calories.

SWEET AND SOUR BLUES

2 FILLETS - CUT INTO 3X3" PIECES

~ SAUCE

1/2 CUP SUGAR	4 TBS SOY SAUCE
1/3 CUP VINEGAR	2 CUPS WATER
3 TBS SHERRY	4 TBS CORNSTARCH
	1 YSP SALT

4 TBS MINCED GINGER
3 SCALLIONS - CHOPPED

MIX ALL INGREDIENTS FOR SAUCE, EXCEPT GINGER & SCALLIONS. DREDGE FISH IN FLOUR. FRY IN VERY HOT OIL, 1/2" DEEP, IN A LARGE SKILLET - FOR 2 MIN. EACH SIDE. LOWER HEAT AND COOK 2 MIN. MORE EACH SIDE. RAISE HEAT AND COOK 1 MIN. MORE EACH SIDE. THE FISH SHOULD BE QUITE CRISP NOW. KEEP WARM IN 150° OVEN, BUT NO LONGER THAN 10 MIN. OR FISH WILL LOSE IT'S CRISPNESS. POUR OFF ALL BUT 1 TBS OIL. SAUTÉ GINGER & SCALLIONS. ADD SAUCE & COOK UNTIL TRANSLUCENT, 3-5 MIN. POUR OVER FISH & SERVE.

BLUEFISH BAKED IN CREAM

2 FILLETS
3/4 CUP HEAVY CREAM
BUTTER
CHOPPED PARSLEY
SALT and PEPPER

PREHEAT OVEN TO 375.°

Place bluefish skin side down on a greased baking dish. DOT with BUTTER AND BAKE ABOUT 15 minutes. Add CREAM AND BAKE 10 minutes more - BASTING with PAN JUICES. SEASON with SALT and PEPPER. SERVE with CHOPPED parsley AND PAN JUICES.

BRIAN'S BLUES

2 FILLETS
1/3 CUP BUTTER
1 tsp minced garlic
1 CUP IMPORTED BEER
   CORNSTARCH

3 TBS HEAVY CREAM
2 tsp BASIL
1 tsp PAPRIKA
   SALT & PEPPER
   BROWN RICE - COOKED

RUB FILLETS WITH SALT & PEPPER, LET STAND A
FEW MINUTES. HEAT BUTTER IN A LARGE SKILLET.
ADD GARLIC and HEAT UNTIL garlic sizzles.
ADD BEER and bring TO a simmer. ADD FISH,
SKIN SIDE DOWN. COVER. BASTE FREQUENTLY.
WHEN FISH IS DONE, PLACE ON A BED OF BROWN
RICE. ADD CREAM and SEASONINGS to JUICES IN
PAN. THICKEN WITH A FEW SPRINKLES OF CORN-
STARCH. POUR OVER FILLETS and SPRINKLE WITH
PAPRIKA.

HONEY - DIPPED BLUEFISH CHEEKS

1/2 CUP BUTTER	1/2 FRESH LEMON
1-2 lbs. Fresh BLUEFISH CHEEKS	3 TBS HONEY
3/4 CUP White Flour	2 EGGS
1/4 cup cornmeal	1 TBS WATER
	2 TBS Fresh MINT

HEAT butter over low FLAME iN HEAVY frying Pan. Do not allow to burn. Place cheeks in colander and squeeze the lemon over them - Drain - (Do not rinse with water. It will destroy the Flavor). Lightly bEAT EGGS & water & Honey in A flat bowl. fill a brown Paper bag with flour and cornmeal. COAT CHEEKS with Honey mixture and shake in bag of Flour and cornmeal. fry in the butter (Just below the burning point) until golden brown - turning Only once. Drain on paper towel. Serve Hot, sprinkled with mint and lemon Juice.

NOTES:

Some people like A HEAVY batter, therefore double dipping is suggested. Blue fish cheeks are the most DELECTABLE part of the fish and usually sell for much less than the fillets. You may also use this RECIPE on fillets cut into finger-size pieces for fish sticks or into bite-size pieces for Hors d'oeuvres.

JEAN'S BLUEFISH WITH SOUR CREAM

2 FILLETS

   SALT and PEPPER

1½ CUPS SOUR CREAM

½ CUP MAYONNAISE

3 TBS CHOPPED CHIVES

3 TBS LEMON JUICE

PREHEAT OVEN TO 375°.

DRY FILLETS AND RUB WITH SALT and PEPPER. ARRANGE IN BUTTERED CASSEROLE (PREFERABLY ON EARTHENWARE BAKING dish). MIX CREAM, MAYONNAISE CHIVES and LEMON JUICE. SEASON WITH SALT and PEPPER. SPREAD OVER FILLETS. BAKE 20 MINUTES. PLACE UNDER BROILER TO BROWN.

Liz's Bluefish Pudding - Nordic style

2 Fillets	3 cups HALF & HALF
1 cup converyed Rice	BAY LEAF
2 cups milk	1 TBS worcestershire
3 Eggs	1/2 tsp grated nutmeg

PREHEAT OVEN TO 350°.

Heat the HALF & HALF with 1 tsp salt, bay LEAF and the Worcestershire sauce. Add the Fillets, cover and simmer slowly for 20 minutes or until fish is Flaky and tender. Allow Fish to cool in the sauce.

MEANWHILE bring the milk to Almost a boil in the Top of a DOUBLE Boiler. Add the rice, REDUCE the HEAT AND COOK for 25 min. or until most of the milk is absorbed. BlEnd the EGGS with the Rice, Adding the nutmeg and 1 cup of the liquid in which the Fish was cooked. Bone and Flake the fish FINELy and

add to the Rice mixture. Place in a well-greased baking dish. Bake for 50-60 minutes.
Serve with lingonberries or whole cranberry sauce.

MOUSSE DE BLUEFISH

1½ lbs. BLUEFISH - COOKED
2 CUPS LIGHT CREAM
5 EGGS
4 EGG WHITES

2 TBS BUTTER- MELTED
SALT & WHITE PEPPER
3 CUPS HOLLANDAISE
(SEE SAUCES)

PREHEAT OVEN TO 350°

In a blender combine fillets, eggs, egg whites, butter and half the cream. Blend until smooth. Combine with rest of cream. Add salt and pepper and transfer to a 2qt. casserole. Place in a pan of water and bake uncovered for 45 minutes or until a knife inserted in center comes out clean. Serve with Hollandaise sauce.

FRENCH BLUE SANDWICH

BLUEFISH SALAD (SEE PAGE 22 - OMIT ALFALFA SPROUTS)

8 SLICES OF BREAD - 4 SANDWICHES
2 EGGS
1/4 CUP CREAM
PINCH OF NUTMEG
SALT & PEPPER
BUTTER

MAKE FOUR SANDWICHES FROM THE BLUEFISH SALAD.
BEAT THE EGGS SLIGHTLY WITH THE CREAM, AND ADD
THE SEASONINGS. DIP SANDWICHES IN THE EGG
MIXTURE. FRY IN BUTTER UNTIL GOLDEN ON BOTH
SIDES.

SERVES 4

BLUEFISH FLORENTINE

1 1/2 CUPS PURÉED SPINACH OR 2 BOXES FROZEN
                                CHOPPED SPINACH
2 FILLETS
   FLOUR   2 TBS OLIVE OIL
   SALT & PEPPER   MORNAY SAUCE
                             PARMESAN CHEESE

HEAT OIL IN FRYING PAN. DIP FILLETS IN SEASONED
FLOUR AND BROWN IN OIL ON BOTH SIDES. PLACE
SPINACH IN A GREASED SHALLOW BAKING DISH. PLACE
FILLETS ON TOP OF SPINACH. COVER WITH MORNAY SAUCE
and SPRINKLE WITH PARMESAN CHEESE. BROIL UNTIL
CHEESE IS bubbly.

∿ MORNAY SAUCE

2 TBS BUTTER   3/4 CUP CREAM
1 1/2 TBS FLOUR   1 EGG YOLK - bEATEN
    PINCH OF NUTMEG, SALT & PEPPER

OVER MEDIUM HEAT MELT BUTTER and add FLOUR. STIR A
FEW MINUTES, THEN gradually ADD CREAM. STIR UNTIL THICK-
ENED. Add SEASONINGS. Add a SMALL AMOUNT OF SAUCE to
THE EGG YOLK, THEN RETURN MIXTURE to THE SAUCE, UNTIL HEATED.

SMOKED BLUEFISH

2 FILLETS
   SALT and PEPPER
   Wood Chips (Preferably Hickory)

Soak the wood chips overnight in water. Place a
double layer of charcoal in the fire pit of your
smoker and burn until gray. Put a single layer of
chips on the coals and wait until they are
smoking well. Place a pan of water over the coals
and smoking chips, and place the seasoned fillets,
skin side down, on the grill in the smoker. Cover
and smoke at least 8 hours. Approximately
every two hours stir coals and place another
layer of chips on.

    If you have no commercially made smoker,
take a metal garbage can and fill the
bottom with 1-inch layer of sand. At the

TOP LEVEL OF SAND - PUNCH FOUR HOLES, THE SIZE OF
DIMES, IN THE CAN. PLACE THE COALS ON THE
SAND. PIERCE SIDES OF THE CAN ABOUT A FOOT
ABOVE THE BED OF COALS AND PUT 2 METAL
RODS THROUGH THE CAN, TO PROVIDE SUPPORT FOR THE
METAL BASIN OF WATER. REPEAT SAME, FOR SUPPORT
FOR YOUR GRILL - 8-10 INCHES ABOVE WATER BASIN.
USE THE CAN COVER AS A TOP. THE WATER KEEPS
THE FISH COOL AND MOIST WHILE THE SMOKE HAS
ITS EFFECT ON THE MEAT.
* *
     FOR A SUPERB, DRYER SMOKED FISH, SOAK
THE FILLETS OVER NIGHT, IN A GLASS OR CERAMIC
DISH, IN JOHN'S BRINE.
  ~ BRINE

2 QUARTS WATER   ½ CUP LEMON JUICE
1 CUP noniodized salt   ¼ TBS GARLIC POWDER
½ CUP BROWN SUGAR   1 tsp ONION POWDER

AFTER SOAKING IN THE BRINE, WASH THE FILLETS
THOROUGHLY IN WATER AND PAT DRY BEFORE SMOKING.

COLD BLUEFISH POACHED WITH SORREL SAUCE

2 FILLETS
SORREL SAUCE
    (SEE SAUCES)

Wrap each fillet in aluminum foil and place in a large skillet over medium HEAT. Add Enough water to the pan to barely cover fillets. Cover skillet and bring water to a boil. Reduce HEAT and simmer for About 20-25 minutes. Serve cold with sorrel sauce.

Great for a luncheon or summer supper.

BLUEFISH with GIN

2 FILLETS
½ CUP GIN

PREHEAT OVEN TO 375°.

Place fillets in buttered casserole. Cover with gin.
Bake for 20 minutes.

Bluefish Fritters

2 cups cooked, finely chopped fish
1 onion - minced
1 TBS melted butter
1 Egg - beaten slightly
1/2 tsp baking powder
  Flour (about 1/2 cup)
  Oil for frying
  Clam broth - optional

Mix all ingredients, using enough flour to hold
together (if necessary to thin, use clam
broth or fish stock). Refrigerate for an hour.
Drop tablespoons of batter into 1/2" of hot
oil in a heavy frying pan (or deep fry).
Fry slowly, turning once. Drain on a paper
towel and keep warm.

Serve with catsup.

BLUEFISH Andros Island style

2 FILLETS
24 ozs Clam Broth or Fish stock
1 CARROT
1 BAY LEAF

1/2 cup white wine
1/2 cup white vinegar
3 LEMONS
3 EGG yolks

In a fish poacher or kettle, bring the broth, carrot, bay leaf, wine and vinegar to a boil. Add the fillets (no need for a rack) and enough water to barely cover the fish. Cover and poach for 10-15 minutes (10 minutes per inch thickness of fillet at the thickest part). Beat the egg yolks in a bowl until frothy. Add the juice of the 3 lemons. Remove the fish from the broth, cut into about six pieces and place in a soup tureen. Add a few tablespoons of the broth to the egg mixture — to be sure the egg won't cook in the Hot liquid. Then stir all the broth and Egg mixture together and pour over the fish. Serve immediately in large soup bowls and accompany with French bread. Do not reheat, as egg will become cooked.

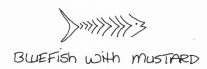

BLUEFISH WITH MUSTARD

2 FILLETS
DIJON MUSTARD

PREHEAT OVEN TO 375°.

Place fish in greased baking dish. Spread a generous (do not skimp) coat of mustard over top of fillets. Bake for 20 minutes or until fish flakes easily with a fork.

LEMON and GARLIC BLUES

2 FILLETS
3 OR 4 CLOVES OF GARLIC
1/2 CUP LEMON JUICE
1/2 CUP SHERRY
3 TBS BUTTER

PREHEAT OVEN TO 375°

PRESS the GARLIC CLOVES and add the fine pressings to the lemon juice and sherry. Marinate the fillets in this mixture for 15 minutes. Then bake the fillets for 20-25 minutes. Simmer the marinade in a saucepan for several minutes to cook the garlic. Add the butter and pour the sauce over fillets just before serving.

COLD POACHED WHOLE BLUEFISH

1 WHOLE BLUEFISH, 4-5 lbs.	2 RIBS CELERY
2 CUPS WHITE VINEGAR	1 tsp DILL
2 CUPS DRY WHITE WINE	2 tsp MIXED HERBS
2 CARROTS	CLOVES

Use a fish poacher (or kettle with a rack on the bottom, large enough for length of fish). Wrap fish in cheesecloth for easy removal from poacher. Put wrapped fish aside. Boil other ingredients with about 3 quarts of water, covered, for 20 minutes. Add fish. Cover and simmer until done, about 20 minutes. Remove fish and carefully peel away skin. Cover with plastic wrap and refrigerate several hours. Discard the poaching liquid and the vegetables. Serve surrounded by cold cooked vegetables and a choice of sauce.

ED'S BLUEFISH SALAD

2 fillers, cooked & flaked	2 cups alfalfa sprouts
4 Ribs celery	Salt & pepper
6 Scallions	tomato-yogurt sauce (SEE sauces)

Dice the scallions and celery and mix with other ingredients. Season to taste. Serve in scooped-out tomatoes on a bed of lettuce or as a sandwich on dark bread. May also be used as canapés on small toasted Rounds or crackers.

BLUE ON BLUE

2 FILLETS
1/4 Lb BLUE CHEESE - CRUMBLED
1/2 cup fine Bread crumbs

PREHEAT OVEN TO 375°.

Place fillets in a greased shallow baking pan.
BAKE FOR 10 MINUTES. REMOVE FROM OVEN.
COVER FILLETS with the CHEESE and TOP with the
BREAD CRUMbs. BAKE ANOTHER 10-15 MINUTES OR
UNTIL fillets are TENDER and CHEESE is MELTED.

WENDY'S BLUEFISH WITH SOY SAUCE

2 FILLETS

1 MEDIUM ONION - SLICED

⅛ CUP SOY SAUCE

1 CAN WHOLE TOMATOES

JUICE OF ½ A LEMON

2 tsp MIXED HERBS

½ GREEN PEPPER - SLICED

⅓ CUP PITTED BLACK OLIVES

PREHEAT OVEN TO 375°.

Line a shallow baking dish with sliced onions.
Place fillets, skin side down, on onions. Rub soy
sauce into fillets. Arrange Tomatoes, cut in half,
green peppers and olives on top of fillets. Pour
½ of the tomato juice over fish. Squeeze the
lemon over all and season to taste. Bake
15-20 minutes.

PLANKED BLUEFISH - CONNECTICUT RIVER STYLE

Fish Fillets
BACON
PAPRIKA

~ Sauce
2 PARTS OLIVE OIL   garlic (OPTIONAL)
1 PART LEMON JUICE   SALT + PEPPER
        OR ANY BOTTLED OIL & VINEGAR DRESSING

These bluefish are baked in front of an open
fire, great for a cookout. LAY FILLETS ON AN
oak board or any other hardwood (do not use
pine or any softwoods). Top each fillet with a
slice of bacon. Using large-head nails about
1½" in length (Roofing nails work well), nail the
fillets to the board, securing the bacon. Nail
two nails in the Top and Two in the bottom.

Leave enough of the nail heads out so that they can be easily removed. Brush each fillet generously with the sauce and sprinkle each with paprika. When the fire is roaring, place the boards about 18" away and at a 60° angle away from the fire. Cook for 40 minutes, turning board upside-down after 20 minutes. Remove nails with the claw of a Hammer, being careful not to burn fingers on the Hot Boards. Wear Heavy mitts.

BLUEFISH STEAKS

1 1/2" THICK STEAKS - CUT ACROSS THE SPINE
OF A FRESH BLUEFISH - LIKE SALMON STEAKS
SALT & FRESHLY GROUND PEPPER

Place steaks in a 2-sided Hamburger grill
and cook over charcoal until golden brown.
Cook about 15 minutes each side, turning constantly
to prevent burning.

BLUEFISH WITH SHALLOT BUTTER AND PINE NUTS

2 FILLETS
1/8 LB BUTTER (1/2 A STICK) - SOFTENED
3 TBS finely chopped shallots
2 TBS PINE NUTS
1/2 CUP FINE BREAD CRUMBS
   SALT & PEPPER

PREHEAT OVEN TO 375.°

MIX SOFTENED BUTTER WITH THE SHALLOTS, PARSLEY,
PINE NUTS, BREAD CRUMBS, SALT and PEPPER.
COVER FILLETS WITH this mixture and BAKE
20-25 MINUTES.

   SERVE WITH LEMON WEDGES.

                        SERVES 5-6

Ruths' Rice-Stuffed Whole Bluefish

1 whole Bluefish - 4-5 lbs.	3 TBS Chopped Parsley
2 cups Rice	3 TBS Chopped Dill
4 cups Clam broth	1 cup chopped onion
2 TBS Butter	1 cup finely chopped celery

1 cup SEEDLESS CURRANTS - SOAKED IN 1/2 CUP WHITE
1/2 CUP PINENUTS or SUNFLOWER SEEDS.   WINE.

∿ Basting Liquid

JUICE OF 1 LEMON	2 TBS Parsley
1 CUP WHITE WINE	2 TBS DILL
1/2 CUP OLIVE OIL	

PREHEAT OVEN TO 375°

COOK RICE IN CLAM broth. Sauté ONIONS, CELERY, dill, and parsley in butter UNTIL tender. mix IN rice, currants and NUTS. Stuff fish. Place ANY LEFTOVER stuffing IN A SEPARATE casserole Dish. SKEWER fish and lace closed. Place IN pan and pour

basting liquid over fish. Bake for an hour. Place
the extra stuffing in the oven At the same time
and serve with the fish.

BLUEFISH DIFFERENT

2 FILLETS

Wrap bluefish fillets separately and tightly in foil. Place wrapped fish in upper rack of dishwasher. Use NO soap but run washer through its complete cycle.
Serve with tartar sauce and lemon wedges.

FISHERMAN BILL'S FAVORITE

2 FILLETS - WITH DARK MEAT REMOVED
3 ONIONS - SLICED
1 CAN CREAM OF CELERY SOUP - UNDILUTED

PREHEAT OVEN TO 375°.

PLACE SLICED ONIONS ON THE BOTTOM OF A BUTTERED CASSEROLE OR BAKING DISH. LAY FILLETS ON TOP OF ONIONS AND COVER WITH THE CELERY SOUP. BAKE FOR 20 MINUTES OR UNTIL FISH FLAKES EASILY WITH A FORK.

BLUEFISH CAKES

1 FILLET - COOKED & FLAKED
4 MEDIUM POTATOES
2 ONIONS
2 EGGS   SALT + PEPPER
2/3 CUP MAYONNAISE   BUTTER OR VEG. OIL

PEEL, COOK, AND MASH POTATOES. CHOP ONIONS AND
SAUTÉ THEM IN BUTTER OR OIL UNTIL GOLDEN. MIX
FISH, POTATOES, ONIONS, EGGS, MAYONNAISE AND
SPICES TOGETHER. FORM INTO PATTIES. COOK IN
FRYING PAN IN BUTTER OR OIL UNTIL BROWN, TURNING
ONCE. SERVE WITH TOMATO-YOGURT SAUCE (SEE
SAUCES) OR KETCHUP.

When formed into bite-size balls, these may
be served as canapés with choice of sauce.

BLUEFISH WITH TOPPING

2 FILLETS
1/2 LEMON

SHREDDED WHEAT
BUTTER

PREHEAT OVEN TO 375°.

SQUEEZE LEMON OVER FILLETS. PLACE IN GREASED BAKING DISH. GRIND SHREDDED WHEAT IN A BLENDER (OR PULVERIZE WITH A ROLLING PIN). MAKE ENOUGH CRUMBS TO MAKE A GENEROUS TOPPING. PLACE OVER FILLETS. DOT WITH BUTTER. BAKE 20 MINUTES OR UNTIL FISH FLAKES EASILY WITH A FORK. SERVE WITH LEMON WEDGES AND PARSLEY.

COLD CURED BLUEFISH OR BLOX

2 FRESH FILLETS	2 TBS ground PEPPer
4 BUNCHES OF DILL	2/3 CUP SALT
2 TBS ground ALLSPICE	2/3 cup sugar

Rub the Flesh of the FILLETS thoroughly with SALT, sugar and ALLSpice. Place one FILLET, SKIN side down, ON A bed OF DILL IN A glass or CERAMIC Dish or platter that has sides AT LEAST 1/2 inch High. COVER with DILL AND place the SECOND FILLET Flesh side down on top to make A SANDwich. SPRINKLE with REMAINING SALT mixture AND COVER with the REST OF THE DILL. COVER PLATTER with plastic WRAP. Place A boArd ON Top AND AdditionAL weights AS WELL (such AS STones) AND REFRIGERATE FOR AT LEAST 48 Hours but PREFERABLY 3-4 dAys.

TURN the SANDWICH ONCE EVERY 12 HOURS. DO
NOT DISCARD the JUICE, AS IT AIDS IN the
CURING. WHEN READY TO SERVE, DISCARD the
JUICE AND DILL AND SCRAPE THE SPICES OFF THE
FLESH. SLICE THINLY AND HORIZONTALLY to the
SKIN. SERVE AS YOU WOULD LOX, WITH CREAM
CHEESE, bagels OR DARK BREAD, LEMON WEDGES
AND/OR MUSTARD DILL SAUCE (SEE SAUCES), OR
AS CANAPÉS ON SMALL TOASTED ROUNDS.

EASY BLUEFISH CUSTARD PIE

makes its own crust. Is lighter and more tender than a quiche. Delicious for a quickie lunch or supper.

½ cup chopped cooked bluefish
1 small green pepper - seeded & chopped
1 small onion - chopped
1 clove garlic - minced
8-10 mushrooms - sliced
1 TBS butter
½ cup Bisquick
1½ cups milk

3 eggs
2 TBS soft butter

PREHEAT OVEN TO 375°.

Sauté green peppers & onions in 1 TBS butter until limp. Add garlic & mushrooms and sauté a few minutes longer. Add fish.

Put Bisquick, milk, eggs and soft butter in the blender. mix by pushing the first button on- then off. Do not overmix. Add fish & vegetables to blender mixture and pour into a greased 10" pie plate. Bake for 30 minutes or until custard is set. Let stand 5 minutes before serving.

BLUEFISH STEW

1 MEDIUM BLUEFISH OR 2 FILLETS	1 CUP COOKED CORN NIBLETS
2 SMALL ONIONS - CHOPPED	1 CUP COOKED LIMA BEANS
2 TBS FLOUR	SALT & PEPPER
2 TBS BUTTER	WORCESTERSHIRE SAUCE
2 CANS EVAPORATED MILK	1 TBS LEMON JUICE
2 CUPS MILK	

SIMMER FISH IN THE 2 CUPS OF MILK UNTIL WHITE
AND FLAKY. REMOVE FROM PAN, RESERVING LIQUID,
AND CUT INTO BITE-SIZE PIECES. DISCARD SKIN AND
BLACK MEAT. IN A STEW POT SAUTÉ ONIONS IN
THE BUTTER UNTIL GOLDEN. ADD FLOUR, STIR, THEN
GRADUALLY ADD LIQUID FROM THE COOKED FISH, THE
EVAPORATED MILK AND THE FISH PIECES. SIMMER
TEN MINUTES. ADD CORN, LIMA BEANS AND SEASONINGS.
SIMMER 10 MINUTES MORE.

SERVE IN BOWLS WITH OYSTER CRACKERS.

HONEY BLUES

2 FILLETS
1/2 cup LEMON JUICE
1/2 CUP HONEY
1 1/2 OZ. SLICED ALMONDS

PREHEAT OVEN TO 375.°

MARINATE THE FILLETS IN THE MIXED HONEY, LEMON JUICE and ALMONDS FOR 15 MINUTES. BAKE THE FILLETS FOR 20-25 MINUTES, THEN PLACE UNDER THE BROILER FOR A MINUTE TO BROWN THE ALMONDS. JUST BEFORE SERVING, HEAT THE RESERVED MARINADE and POUR OVER THE FILLETS.

ITALIAN STYLE BAKED BLUEFISH

2 FILLETS	1 TBS chopped garlic
1 1/2 lbs POTATOES	1/4 cup chopped parsley
2/3 cup olive oil	SALT & PEPPER

PREHEAT OVEN TO 450°

Peel and slice potatoes. Use a shallow casserole, but one large enough to accommodate fish without overlapping. Put in potatoes and half the olive oil, half the garlic, half the parsley and salt and pepper to taste. Mix well. Spread potatoes evenly to cover dish. Place on the upper rack and bake until potatoes are half done - about 15 minutes. Remove from oven and place fish, skin side down, over potatoes. Baste fish with remaining oil, garlic, parsley and salt and pepper. Return to oven and bake for ten minutes more.

Remove from oven and baste with pan Juices.
Return again to oven for another Ten minutes
or until fish is flaky and Potatoes are
browned.

Blinns & Blues

2 smoked fillets   Lemon Juice
milk   Parsley - Chopped

In a saucepan barely cover fillets with milk.
Bring milk to almost a boil. Reduce heat and
simmer until tender. Make the white sauce.
Flake the fillets with a fork and remove any
bones. Add to the white sauce. Heat, sprinkle
with lemon juice and parsley to taste.
Serve on toast points or rice.

∿ White Sauce

3 TBS butter   1 cup milk or cream
3 TBS Flour

Melt butter over low heat. Add flour and stir for a
few minutes. slowly add milk and stir until thickened.

Small Blues Sautéed with Bacon and Onions

2 small Fillets - 3 lbs or more
4 strips of Bacon
4 scallions - chopped
   milk
   flour (corn meal)
   salt & pepper

In a large frying pan cook bacon until crisp.
Remove, crumble and keep warm. Cook scallions
in bacon grease until limp. Remove and keep
warm. Dip fillets first in the milk, then in
the seasoned flour (or ½ flour, ½ corn meal).
Fry in the bacon grease about 3 minutes on
one side, turn and cook 3 minutes on the
other side or until nicely browned. Top with
bacon and scallions. Serve.

DEVILISH BLUES

2 FILLETS
   MELTED BUTTER
1 CUP GRATED CHEDDAR CHEESE
⅛ tsp Tabasco
1 TBS PREPARED MUSTARD
1 TBS HORSERADISH

BRUSH FILLETS WITH MELTED butter. BROIL 10 MINUTES. MIX ALL OTHER INGREDIENTS. COAT FILLETS WITH MIXTURE AND RETURN TO BROILER UNTIL CHEESE IS MELTED AND BROWNED.

SMOKED BLUEFISH PÂTÉ

4 OZ. SMOKED FISH
4 OZ. CREAM CHEESE
1 SMALL ONION - CHOPPED FINE
1½ TBS LEMON JUICE

Combine all the ingredients in a blender and blend until smooth. Garnish with a few sprigs of parsley and serve on crackers or melba toast.

BLUEFISH CHOWDER

1 LARGE BLUEFISH OR 2 FILLETS

1 Carrot, cut up   2 celery stalks
1 onion, quartered   3 onions, chopped
1/2 lb bacon or 1/4 lb salt pork
5 medium potatoes - peeled & quartered
1 cup cream
Salt & pepper
paprika

Place fish in water to barely cover fillets.
Add the carrot, onion, and celery stalks.
Poach for 25-30 minutes or till fish is flaky.
Strain. Reserve stock (about 4 cups). Remove fish
from bones, discarding bones and skin. Sauté
Chopped bacon or pork in frying pan till golden.
Add chopped onions and sauté till golden. Remove
from heat. Cook potatoes in stock until tender. Dice

potatoes. Add fish, onions and bacon. Cook
over low heat. Add cream and salt and
pepper to taste. Do not allow to boil. Serve
in a bowl with a pat of butter and a dash
of paprika. For a richer chowder, use
evaporated milk.

Fish Stock

1 Bluefish Carcass - with Head and Tail After Filleting.
½ cup white vinegar
½ cup white wine
2 Carrots
2 Ribs Celery
1 ½ TBS chopped fresh dill or 1 TBS dried dillweed or seeds
2 QTS Water

Simmer Carcass in Water with other ingredients
for 30-40 minutes. Uncover and strain, discarding
bones. Boil down stock, uncovered, for another
½ hour or until ⅔ of the Amount is left.
This stock will keep in the Refrigerator for 2
weeks if boiled every few days. It is a good
base for sauces, soups and Bouillabaisse. The
gel from the stock is good by itself eaten
cold with lemon juice squeezed on top.

ALMOND BLUEFISH HASH

2 CUPS COOKED BLUEFISH
1½ CUPS COOKED, CUBED POTATOES
3 CUPS WHITE SAUCE
1 CUP TOASTED SLIVERED ALMONDS
 BUTTER

PREHEAT OVEN TO 350°.

SAUTÉ ALMONDS IN BUTTER UNTIL GOLDEN.
MAKE WHITE SAUCE AND ADD BLUEFISH &
POTATOES. TRANSFER TO A SHALLOW BAKING DISH.
TOP WITH ALMONDS. BAKE 15 MINUTES OR UNTIL
HEATED through.

~ White Sauce

6 TBS butter   3 CUPS milk

6 TBS Flour   Salt & pepper

MELT BUTTER OVER LOW HEAT. Add Flour and stir
FOR A FEW MINUTES. SLOWLY Add milk and stir
UNTIL THICKENED, 5 OR 10 MINUTES.

BAKED MARINATED BLUEFISH

2 FILLETS	1 BAY LEAF
1 CUP OLIVE OIL	1 tsp SALT
2 CLOVES GARLIC - CRUSHED	1 tsp PEPPER
1 ONION - SLICED	1/4 CUP LEMON JUICE

DRY WHITE WINE

Lay fillets in shallow dish and cover with mixture of oil, garlic, onion, bay leaf, salt, pepper, lemon juice and enough wine to cover fish. Allow fish to marinate at least 12 hours.

Remove fish from marinade. Bake fish at 350° for 10 minutes per inch thickness and use marinade for basting.

BLUEFISH CAPERS

2 FILLETS
4 TBS BUTTER
1 TBS LEMON JUICE
2 tsps CAPERS

PREHEAT OVEN TO 350.°

Place FILLETS IN A GREASED baking dish and bake for 20 minutes or UNTIL fish FLAKES EASILY WITH A FORK. In a SKILLET MELT buffer UNTIL brown. Quickly add LEMON JUICE and CAPERS AND COOK FOR 15 SECONDS. Pour over FILLETS and SERVE.

BLUEFISH AU GRATIN

2 FILLETS
2 MEDIUM ONIONS - CHOPPED
1 Cup thinly sliced mushrooms
1 Cup grated SWISS CHEESE
3 TBS BUTTER

PREHEAT OVEN TO 350°

Place fillets, skin side down, in a greased baking dish and Bake 20 minutes. Sauté onions and mushrooms in Butter, then place over baked fillets. Top with grated cheese and place under Broiler until CHEESE is melted and golden brown.

BLUELLABASE - BOUILLABASE

1 Fillet- raw or cooked, cut into medium-size pieces
Fillets of other kinds of fish or mixture of fish and
shellfish - about 3 cups
2 onions - chopped
2 cloves garlic - minced   ½ can tomato Paste
¼ cup olive oil
3 tomatoes- chopped
¼ tsp: oregano, Basil, Thyme, Sage, marjoram
1½ Qts. Fish Stock   or   { 24 oz. Clam Juice
                             { 24 oz. Water

Sauté onion and garlic in oil in a large Pan. When
golden add tomatoes, Paste and herbs. Cook until
tomatoes are soft. Then add remaining ingredients
and simmer for 20 minutes (be sure shellfish
are well scrubbed before adding). Cooking time
will vary depending on the use of Raw or
cooked fish. Serve with crisp French Bread
and grated Parmesan Cheese.

OPEN-FACED SANDWICH

TOAST BREAD SLICES ON ONE SIDE. COVER UNTOASTED side with BLUEFISH SALAD (SEE RECIPE FOR EO'S BLUEFISH SALAD - page 22 , OMITTING THE ALFALFA SPROUTS).

SPREAD MAYONNAISE EVENLY OVER THE BLUEFISH SALAD. SHAKE GRATED PARMESAN CHEESE OVER MAYONNAISE and place UNDER bROILER UNTIL top is bROWNED and bubbly.

GOOBER BLUES

2 FILLETS
1 CUP COARSELY CHOPPED SALTED PEANUTS
1/4 CUP MELTED BUTTER

PREHEAT OVEN TO 375.°

PLACE FILLETS IN GREASED, SHALLOW CASSEROLE DISH. COVER WITH CHOPPED PEANUTS. DRIBBLE MELTED BUTTER OVER ALL. BAKE FOR 20 - 25 MINUTES. SERVE WITH FRIED BANANAS.

BLUES À L'ORANGE

2 FILLETS

⌣ BASTING SAUCE : ⅓ PART ORANGE JUICE
                    ⅓ PART MELTED BUTTER
                    ⅓ PART SOY SAUCE

PREPARE basting sauce. Place FILLETS, SKin side down, on BROILER PAN. Baste generously with Sauce. Grill under broiler for 20-25 minutes or until done, basting occasionally with Sauce.

LEFTOVER SAUCE is ALSO good on BROILED chicken.

BLUEFISH WITH GINGER AND SCALLIONS

2 FILLETS
1/2 - 3/4 CUP SOY SAUCE
1/4 CUP minced fresh garlic
OR 3 TBS ground ginger
1/2 CUP chopped scallions

PREHEAT OVEN TO 350°

marinate FILLETS IN SOY SAUCE FOR 10 MINUTES
EACH SIDE. THEN RUB FLESH WITH ginger and
SCALLIONS. Place FILLETS IN GREASED baking
dish. Pour soy sauce over FILLETS and
bake 20 MINUTES or UNTIL DONE.

BlUE - AgrEE

2 cups COOKED RICE
2 cups Cooked, flaked bluefish
4 Hard-cooked eggs - chopped
2 TBS minced parsley
1/2 cup MELTED Butter

ADD TO THE Hot COOKED RICE the REST OF the INgrEDIENTS, EXCEpt the Butter. PrEHEAT iN the top OF A DOUBLE boiler. Add MELTED Butter and stir iN WELL.

Bluefish with Shrimp Sauce

2 Fillets
1 can Cream of Shrimp soup
1/3 cup Chopped Cooked Shrimp
OR 1 2/3 - 3 oz can of Tiny Shrimp
1/2 cup White Wine
1 Lemon

PREHEAT OVEN TO 350°

Place Fillets, Skin side Down, in a greased Baking dish and cover with remaining mixed ingredients, including the Juice from the lemon. Slice the squeezed lemon into thin HALF-Rounds and decoratively place in a line on Fillets. Bake 25 minutes or until done.

Serve with Rice.

BAKED STUFFED BLUEFISH

2 large fillets or whole fish
2 cups bread crumbs *
1 large onion
4 TBS butter
1/2 lb. chopped mushrooms **

1/2 tsp thyme
1/4 cup chopped parsley
2 TBS chopped celery
LEAVES
1 tsp salt
1 egg - beaten

PREHEAT OVEN TO 375°

Sauté onions in butter until soft. Add the other ingredients and mix well. Stuff the bluefish by placing one fillet over the other. Place in a greased baking dish and bake for 40 minutes or until fish flakes easily with a fork.

* or Pepperidge farms - Arnold stuffing
** try substituting oysters or shrimp

BLUEFISH - SWEDISH STYLE

2 FILLETS
2 Cups White Sauce
  DILL

PREHEAT OVEN TO 350°

Bake the fillets in oven for 20-25 minutes or until just tender. Meanwhile make the white sauce. Add finely chopped fresh dill (or dried dill weed) very generously. Be sure to make it taste Dilly! Serve with a light coating of the sauce. Place the remaining in a dish and serve separately.

.∩ White Sauce

4 TBS Butter   2 cups milk
4 TBS Flour   Salt & pepper

Melt butter over low heat. Add flour and stir a moment. Slowly add milk and stir until thickened. Season with salt and pepper.

FABULOUS MARINATED BLUEFISH
~ AND ~
COLD PASTA BLUEFISH SALAD

The following recipes are Chef Vannerson's favorites. The first makes a fabulous marinated bluefish, and the second is a salad using the leftover marinade and leftover bluefish. She says that they are "great for a crowd, and both can be made ahead of time."

~

2 BLUEFISH FILLETS (OR MORE DEPENDING ON SIZE)
1 RED ONION, SLICED
2 TOMATOES, SLICED

~ MARINADE

1 CUP OLIVE OIL
1/2 CUP RED WINE VINEGAR
1/2 CUP DIJON MUSTARD
2 TABLESPOONS SUGAR

1 TEASPOON SALT
4 TABLESPOONS CHOPPED PARSLEY
1 1/2 TEASPOONS FRESH GROUND PEPPER

3/4 CUP VODKA OR GIN (OMIT IF MAKING ONLY THE SALAD)

Mix all the ingredients for marinade except the vodka or gin. Puree in blender. Stir in vodka or gin.

Place the fillets, skin side down, in pyrex bowl (not metal) and pour marinade over them. Cover with plastic wrap and refrigerate for two to four hours. Turn the fish over in the marinade every hour or so.

Remove fillets, reserving the marinade (for use in accompanying recipe), and place them, skin side down, on a broiling pan that has been lined with foil.

Broil for five minutes at 5-6 inches from heat. Remove and top with the sliced tomatoes and red onion. Broil again until fish is flaked and vegetables are cooked. Sprinkle with chopped parsley.

COLD PASTA BLUEFISH SALAD

1 POUND PASTA IN DIFFERENT SHAPES
BLUEFISH MARINADE
LEFTOVER MARINATED BLUEFISH
2 TABLESPOONS CAPERS
4 TABLESPOONS CHOPPED PARSLEY
2 TABLESPOONS CHOPPED CHIVES
1 CUP CHERRY TOMATOES, QUARTERED
1 TABLESPOON CHOPPED SUN-DRIED TOMATOES
1/2 CUP CHOPPED SEEDED CUCUMBER (OPTIONAL)
MINCED FRESH PARSLEY FOR GARNISH

COOK A VARIETY OF PASTA SHAPES, ALL
APPROXIMATELY THE SAME SIZE (ZITI, SPIRALS,
SHELLS, PINWHEELS, ETC.). COOK UNTIL AL DENTE,
THEN WHILE STILL WARM, TOSS WITH THE
BLUEFISH MARINADE. USE A GENEROUS
AMOUNT OF THE MARINADE, AS THE PASTA
SHOULD NOT BE DRY.

TOSS WITH THE bluefish, THE CAPErs, the chopped PARSLEY, the Chives, the tomatoes, AND the cucumber. Place IN refrigerator FOR one Hour. SErve ON LETTuce WITH fresh PARSLEY (OR WATER-CRESS) AND LEMON WEDGES.

FROM the Thisxie REStaurant, NANTUCKET; SHARON VANNErson, Chef DE CUISINE.

BAKED BLUEFISH
(A GAY HEAD RECIPE)

½ loaf DAY-old Home-STYLE Bread, CrUSTS Removed

1½ teaspoons poultry seasoning

½ cup ground SALT Pork

¼ teaspoon Freshly ground Pepper

1 Tablespoon melted Butter

½ cup boiling WATEr

4 BLUEFISH FILLETS, a total of approximately 3 pounds

8 lemon slices

8 thin slices SALT Pork

Additional lemon slices (optional)

Parsley sprigs

Preheat oven to 375° F.

Prepare the bread stuffing as follows: cut the bread into ½-inch cubes. In a mixing bowl combine the bread, poultry seasoning, ground SALT pork, pepper, and melted butter. Using a fork for mixing, gradually add the boiling WATEr, lifting and combining all ingredients, until properly moistened. Spread The stuffing equally on two of the bluefish fillets; cover with the remaining fillets. Place 8 lemon slices on the fish, then the thin salt pork slices.

BAKE the fish in a shallow casserole or baking dish (try lining with aluminum foil for easy cleanup) about 25 minutes. The fish is ready for the table when it flakes easily when pierced with a fork. Serve with additional lemon slices, if desired, and garnish with parsley sprigs.

From the Martha's Vineyard Cook Book (The Globe Pequot Press, 1971) by Louise Tate King and Jean Stewart Wexler.

SPICY BLUEFISH WITH SUMMER SAVORY

6 very small BLUEFISH FILLETS
FLOUR
Enough Oil to sauté
SALT, PEPPER, FRESH SUMMER SAVORY TO TASTE

≈ SAUCE

3 TABLESPOONS OLIVE OIL

1 MEDIUM-SIZE ONION, DICED

1 JALAPEÑO PEPPER, DICED

28 OUNCES CANNED TOMATOES IN JUICE, OR FRESH SUMMER TOMATOES

8 OUNCES WHITE WINE

8 OUNCES CLAM JUICE (MORE MAY BE NEEDED)

1 BAY LEAF

≈ GARNISH

1 YELLOW BELL PEPPER
1 GREEN BELL PEPPER
1 RED BELL PEPPER
2 CUPS FIRM MUSHROOMS

To make SAUCE, SAUTÉ ONION AND JALAPEÑO

pepper in the 3 tablespoons of oil for a few minutes. Add white wine and simmer over medium heat for 5 minutes. Add 8 ounces clam juice, tomatoes, and bay leaf; simmer for 45 minutes. Puree sauce through a food mill. The sauce should be just thick enough to cover the fish lightly. If it is too thick, lighten it with more clam juice or white wine. If too thin, simmer until it is reduced to the desired consistency.

-To make garnish, roast the peppers—rub them with a little olive oil and put them under a very hot broiler and char the skin until black. Rub skin off under running water. Discard seeds and stems. Cut mushrooms & peppers into 1/4" dice.

-To complete the dish, lightly dredge bluefish in flour. Put some oil in a frying pan,

enough to cover the bottom. ADD BLUEFISH.
Sauté, then place on Platter and KEEP
WARM. Add DICED mushrooms to the oil,
ADDING extra oil if needed, then ADD
peppers. SEASON generously with salt,
pepper, AND fresh summer savory. LADLE
WARM sauce across fish, then spoon
garnish on Top.

SERVES 6

FROM michael shannon's CLUB CAR RESTAURANT,
NANTUCKET (FRANK LUCAS, sous-chef).

NORTH WHARF FISH HOUSE STEW

2 8-OUNCE bluefish fillets, DICED
1 POUND SCALLOPS *
1 POUND langostinos *
1 CUP CHOPPED CELERY
1 CUP CHOPPED CARROT
1 CUP CHOPPED ONION
1/4 TEASPOON CAYENNE PEPPER
1/4 TEASPOON black pepper
PINCH OF BASIL
TAMARI to TASTE
3 TABLESPOONS OLIVE OIL
1 QUART FRESH FISH STOCK (SEE PAGE 49)
1 QUART CLAM BROTH
1 QUART CANNED WHOLE PEELED TOMATOES,
         BROKEN UP
1 CUP PREPARED MARINARA SAUCE
6 MEDIUM-SIZE BOILED NEW POTATOES, DICED

IN A HEAVY STEW POT, SAUTÉ IN THE OLIVE
OIL THE CELERY, THE CARROTS, THE ONION. ADD

the CAYENNE AND black PEPPER, the BASIL,
AND the TAMARI.
ADD the Fish STOCK, the Clam broth, the
tomatoes, AND the MARINARA Sauce. Simmer
UNTIL All the Vegetables ARE Tender.
TO SERVE, Sauté the diced fresh bluefish,
fresh scallops, langostinos* and boiled
new POTATOES AND Add to EACH PORTION
OF stew base.

*
The SCALLOPS AND langostinos CAN be
replaced by AN EQUIVALENT AMOUNT OF other
fish or shellfish.

FROM Rob Mitchell's NORTH WHARF
Fish HOUSE, NANTUCKET.

BLUEFISH WITH APPLES

4 6-ounce bluefish fillets
3 TABLESPOONS UNSALTED BUTTER
1 SMALL RED ONION, thinly SLICED
1 TART APPLE, PEELED AND thinly SLICED
1/2 CUP QUICK FISH STOCK (SEE BELOW)
1/3 CUP HEAVY CREAM
1 to 2 tablespoons Pommery mustard (or any COARSE-grained mustard)
FRESH ITALIAN PARSLEY OR WATERCRESS FOR GARNISH

1. IF YOU ARE PORTIONING the FISH, CUT IT INTO 4 EQUAL PORTIONS, CUTTING slightly ON THE DIAGONAL. DISCARD 2 to 3 INCHES OF THE TAIL END. REMOVE ANY bones. IF THERE IS ANY SKIN ON THE FILLETS, LEAVE IT ON.

2. Reduce the FISH STOCK to 1/4 CUP IN A

1- QUART STAINLESS STEEL SAUCEPAN. SET
ASIDE.

3. PREHEAT A broiler.

4. Butter the bluefish with 1 TABLESPOON
Butter AND place ON AN OILED BROILER PAN.
BROIL the Fish 6 INCHES From the HEAT
UNTIL the top OF The FILLETS IS A light
GOLDEN BROWN. TO CHECK FOR DONENESS,
INSERT A SMALL SHARP KNIfE INTO the
thickEST PART OF EACH FILLET. IF The
FISH IS NOT COOKED through, but ALREADy
brown, turN OFF The broiler AND BAKE
AT 350 DEGREES FOR 3 to 6 MINUTES
UNTIL DONE.

5. meanwhile, heAT 2 TablespooNs butter
IN A 12- INch sauté paN. Add the
ONION AND TOSS over high heAT uNTiL
SOFT. Add the APPLES AND TOSS For
3 minutes. Place ON A serving PlAtter AND

KEEP WARM.

6. Add the REDUCED FISH STOCK to the SAUTÉ PAN. WHISK IN 1 TABLESPOON MUSTARD AND REDUCE the SAUCE to A medium SYRUPY CONSISTENCY. Add the CREAM AND REDUCE UNTIL the SAUCE is thick Enough to COAT A SPOON. ADD SALT, Freshly ground PEPPER, and more mustard to taste.

7. WHEN you remove the FILLETS FROM the broiler pan, do NOT be concerned IF the SKIN stays stuck to the pan. Place the FILLETS over the ONION-APPLE mixture AND top with the SAUCE. GARNISH WITH ITALIAN PARSLEY or WATERCRESS.

FROM <u>ANOTHER SEASON COOKBOOK</u> (THE GLOBE PEQUOT PRESS, 1986) by ODETTE J. BERY, CHEF / OWNER OF ANOTHER SEASON RESTAURANT IN BOSTON.

QUICK FISH STOCK
(FOR USE IN BLUEFISH WITH APPLES)

1 pound haddock, cod, or pollock
2 TABLESPOONS UNSALTED BUTTER
1 SMALL ONION, thinly sliced
1 CELERY STALK, thinly sliced
1/2 BAY LEAF
PINCH OF MACE (OPTIONAL)
FEW SPRIGS PARSLEY (OPTIONAL)
1 CUP WHITE WINE
4 CUPS COLD WATER

1. HEAT the butter IN A 2-3-QUART STAINLESS STEEL OR ENAMEL PAN. (DO NOT USE AN ALUMINUM PAN.) ADD the ONION AND CELERY. GENTLY SAUTÉ over MEDIUM HEAT UNTIL SOFT, being CAREFUL NOT TO BROWN. ADD FISH, BAY LEAF, MACE, PARSLEY, WINE, AND WATER. BRING TO A BOIL AND BOIL FOR 5 MINUTES, then SKIM OFF AND DISCARD ANY FOAM.

2. Gently simmer, uncovered, for 45 minutes, then strain through a fine sieve. (Your cats, if you have any, will love the fish; if not, discard.)

3. If there are a lot of particles in the stock, run it through a couple of layers of cheesecloth to remove them. The stock may be refrigerated 3 to 4 days. Keep fat covering on top of stock. It may also be frozen.

makes 1 quart

From ANOTHER SEASON COOKBOOK (The Globe Pequot Press, 1986) by Odette J. Bery.

BLUEFISH MOLLY'S WAY

2 SLICES bLUEFISH, 8 to 10 OUNCES EACH, WITH SKIN
1/2 CUP SOUR CREAM
2 TEASPOONS WHITE HORSERADISH
1/2 CUP MAYONNAISE
DASH TABASCO SAUCE
DASH WORCESTERSHIRE SAUCE
1/4 TEASPOON GROUND DILL
1 LEMON, CUT IN HALF
FRESH DILL FOR GARNISH

IN A SMALL MIXING bOWL, bEAT SOUR CREAM,
HORSERADISH, MAYONNAISE, TABASCO AND
WORCESTERSHIRE SAUCES, AND GROUND DILL.
PLACE FISH ON bROILER PAN, SKIN SIDE DOWN.
SQUEEZE LEMON HALVES OVER FISH, THEN
SPREAD SAUCE EVENLY OVER EACH PIECE.
WITH FISH ABOUT 8 INCHES FROM bROILER,
HEAT FOR 15 MINUTES. GARNISH WITH FRESH

DILL.

FROM ENTREE LU CATERING COMPANY,
ESSEX, CONNECTICUT.

BEIGNETS DE BLUEFISH

2 POUNDS bluefish FILLETS
1 POUND TOMATOES, PEELED
2 EGGS
FlOUr, SALT, PEPPEr
2 TABLESPOONS OLIVE OIL
1 CUP FISH STOCK

en MARINADE
2 CUPS WATEr
1 TABLESPOON CORIANDER SEED
4 CLOVES GARLIC
1 TABLESPOON CUMIN
3 TABLESPOONS OLIVE OIL

2 hOT PEPPErS
1 WhOLE lEMON PEEL
PINCH OF SAFFRON
2 TABLESPOONS
    GRATED GINGER
6 MINT lEAVES

Blend MARINADE INGREDIENTS XOGether. CuX
FISh INXO thick SCALOPPINES AND place IN
MARINADE. REFRIGErATE FOR A FEW HOUrs.

TO MAKE TOMATO SAUCE, SAUTÉ TOMATOES
IN 1 TABLESPOON OLIVE OIL UNTIL COOKED.
ADD FISH STOCK, 1 CUP MARINADE, AND
SALT TO TASTE. COOK AN ADDITIONAL 15
MINUTES. PUREE IN BLENDER. KEEP WARM.

REMOVE FISH FROM MARINADE AND ADD
SALT and PEPPER. DIP IN FLOUR, THEN IN
BEATEN EGGS. SAUTÉ IN 1 TABLESPOON OLIVE
OIL FOR 2 MINUTES ON EACH SIDE.

SERVE WITH TOMATO SAUCE.

FROM THE CHANTICLEER RESTAURANT,
NANTUCKET — JEAN CHARLES BERRUET,
CHEF/PROPRIETOR.

BLUEFISH WITH ORANGE SAUCE

4 6-ounce bluefish fillets (skin on)
4 tablespoons vegetable oil
2 medium onions, very finely sliced
12 Italian parsley sprigs
1 teaspoon grated orange rind (zest)
2 to 4 tablespoons lemon juice
1/4 cup fresh orange juice
SALT AND PEPPER

Remove any bones from the bluefish.
Just before serving, preheat a broiler
AND ADJUST so that the pan will be 6
inches from the heat.
Brush a broiler PAN AND BLUEFISH with a
little oil and place under the broiler.
While the fish is broiling, heat the 4
teaspoons of vegetable oil in a 10- or 12-

INCH STAINLESS STEEL SAUTÉ PAN. ADD THE ONIONS AND SAUTÉ UNTIL THEY ARE CLEAR BUT STILL SLIGHTLY CRISP. ARRANGE HALF THE ONIONS ON 4 DINNER PLATES AND ARRANGE THE ITALIAN PARSLEY OVER THE ONIONS.

ADD 2 TABLESPOONS LEMON JUICE, THE ORANGE JUICE, AND THE ORANGE ZEST WITH THE REMAINING ONIONS IN THE SAUTÉ PAN AND REDUCE OVER A MEDIUM HEAT FOR 3 TO 5 MINUTES UNTIL THE MIXTURE IS OF A SLIGHTLY SYRUPY CONSISTENCY. ADD SALT AND FRESHLY GROUND BLACK PEPPER TO TASTE AND MORE LEMON JUICE TO TASTE IF DESIRED. WHILE THE SAUCE IS REDUCING, CHECK THE BLUEFISH DONENESS BY INSERTING A SMALL SHARP KNIFE INTO THE THICKEST PART OF THE FISH. IF THE BLUEFISH IS NOT COOKED BUT ALREADY GOLDEN BROWN, FINISH COOKING

by BAKING AT 375 DEGREES FOR ANOTHER
3 to 7 MINUTES.
WHEN THE BLUEFISH IS COOKED, ARRANGE
OVER THE ONIONS AND SPOON THE SAUCE
OVER EACH FILLET. SERVE IMMEDIATELY.

FROM ANOTHER SEASON RESTAURANT IN
BOSTON (ODETTE BERY, CHEF/OWNER).

BlUEFiSh SOUP

8 OUNCES SKINLESS
  bluEfish FiLLET, IN biTE-
  SIZE PiECES

4 SLICES bACON, DiCED

I TABLESPOON bUTTER

½ CUP ChOPPED ONION

I qUART OF
          hALF WATER, hALF
CLAM JUICE, OR PLAIN WATER

2 CUPS ChOPPED CELERY
  (SAVE I TABLESPOON OF LEAVES)

PINCh OF DRIED Xhyme

½ XEASPOON SALT

3 to 4 Turns FreshLy
  groUND PEPPER

I CUP hEAVY CREAM

½ CUP PEELED, SEEDED,
  AND DICED TOMATOES

I TABLESPOON MINCED
  FRESH PARSLEY

1. Fry bACON IN buTTER IN A THICK - boTTomED
4-qUART SAUCE PAN or STOCK poT to RENDER
The FAT. WHEN bACON IS CrISP, REMOVE hALF
OF iT, bIOT ON PAPER XOWElS, AND reserve.
LEAVE bACON FAT AND the OTher hALF OF
The bACON IN The PAN.

2. ADD The ONIONS   AND SAUTÉ UNTIL

lightly browned. ADD Fish stock or other liquid, CELERY, thyme, SALT, AND pepper. Simmer, Covered, 30 to 35 MINUTES, OR UNTIL CELERY IS TENDER.

3. PLACE CONTENTS OF PAN INTO WORK BOWL OF FOOD peocessor, IN TWO batches IF Necessary, AND WORK UNTIL smooth.

4. Return to PAN AND bring to A boil, then lower heat TO Simmer AND ADD CreAM. COOK over low heat 5 MINUTES. ADD TOMATOES AND PARSLEY AND then FISH. SIMMER 3 to 4 MINUTES, AND CORRECT the SEASONING.

5. LADLE the SOUP INTO INDIVIDUAL SOUP PLATES or INTO A SOUP TUREEN. ADD bACON biTS AND CELERY LEAVES AS garNish.

BLUEFISH PROVENÇALE
(BAKED WITH AROMATIC HERBS AND SEASONINGS)

4—5-pound bluefish, CLEANED AND CUT INTO
2-INCH-thick slices ('bone IN)

∿ MARINADE

1 CUP OLIVE OR VEGETABLE
        OIL

1/2 CUP RED WINE VINEGAR

1 TABLESPOON LEMON JUICE

1 teaspoon SALT

1/4 teaspoon Freshly
        ground Pepper

2 CLOVES GARLIC,
        MINCED FINE

Place the bluefish slices IN A shallow
CONTAINER; COMBINE the 1 CUP OIL, Vinegar,
lemon JUICE, 1 teaspoon SALT, PEPPER, AND
The 2 MINCED garlic cloves and pour
over the Fish. MARINATE the Fish IN This
mixTure two to three hours, turning
OCCASIONALLY. REFRIGERATION IS NOT required.
    PREHEAT OVEN TO 450°F.

REMOVE FISH FROM MARINADE; DRY IT thoroughly WITH PAPER TOWELS. DISCARD MARINADE.

2 TABLESPOONS butter

2 TABLESPOONS OlIVE or VEGETABLE OIL

1 CUP ONIONS, thinly sliced

3 CUPS FRESH TOMATOES, CUT IN CHUNKS (CANNED MAY BE SUBSTITUTED)

2 CLOVES GARLIC, MINCED FINE

1 TEASPOON SALT

1/4 TEASPOON FRESHLY ground PEPPER

1 CUP DRY WHITE WINE

4 TABLESPOONS TOMATO PASTE

2 BEEF BOUILLON CUBES

1/2 CUP CHOPPED PARSLEY

1/2 TEASPOON DRIED thyme

SCANT TEASPOON DRIED OREGANO

Over high heat melt the butter with the OIL IN A HEAVY SKILLET UNTIL the butter FOAM subsides. QUICKLY bROWN the Fish ON both SIDES, Allowing 2 to 3 MINUTES per SIDE. Remove from skillet AND ArrAnge IN A shallow FLAMEPROOF bAKING DISH.

IN the SAME SKILLET, OVER MODERATE

heat, cook the onions until transparent. ADD A little more butter or oil if the onions DEMAND IT. ADD The tomatoes, the remaining 2 cloves minced garlic, the remaining teaspoon salt, pepper, wine, tomato paste, bouillon cubes, 1/4 cup of the chopped parsley, thyme, and oregano. Cook over high heat, stirring frequently, about 10 minutes, allowing the liquids to evaporate sufficiently so that sauce is thickened slightly.

Pour the sauce over the bluefish slices, sprinkle with the remaining 1/4 cup chopped parsley, cover the dish tightly with foil, and bake 15 to 20 minutes, or until the fish flakes easily when pierced with a fork.

Transfer the fish to a heated platter; keep warm. Place the baking dish with

Its remaining sauce over high heat and boil rapidly, stirring constantly, until about 2 cups of sauce remain. Pour sauce over fish slices and serve immediately.

NOTE: The sauce may be thickened slightly with a paste of 1 tablespoon flour mixed with 1 tablespoon softened butter.

FROM The MARTHA'S VINEYARD COOKBOOK (The Globe Pequot Press, 1971) by LOUISE TATE KING AND JEAN STEWART WEXLER.

BLOUP

8 quahogs

1/2 gallon WATER

1 Tablespoon bACON Drippings

1 large DICED ONION

5 garlic cloves, SMASHED

10 summer TOMATOES, peeled, seeded, AND chopped

1/4 cup fresh basil, finely chopped

1 Tablespoon Chopped PARSLEY

1 TABlespoon sugar

PiNCH OF THyme

SALT & PEPPer TO TASTE

2 CLOVES

1 BAY LEAF

1 pound bluefish cut into 1" cubes

WASH quahogs; put iNTO SOUP POT With 1 quart OF WATer. Cover AND STEAM UNTil OPENED. RESErVE STOCK; remove meat from shell and chop and Reserve. In heavy-bottomed SOUP POT, melt bACON drippings and add chopped onion and garlic. Sauté until translucent. ADD chopped tomatoes, quahog Juice, seasonings, and remainder OF WATer. Simmer 1 Hour. ADD bluefish cubes. Simmer for 15 minutes. ADD quahog meat, Return to Simmer, AND Serve.

This RECIPE is exceptional in late August when the blues are thick, the tomatoes are Ripe, basil is abundant, and the nights have a faint whisper of autumn.

From E. J. Harvey's The island Restaurant, Nantucket.

BLUEFISH DIJONAISE

2 8- ounce bluefish fillets
2 tablespoons prepared horseradish
2 tablespoons Dijon mustard
2 tablespoons mayonnaise
1 teaspoon old Bay seasoning
½ cup bread crumbs — seasoned

mix Horseradish, mayonnaise, and mustard.
Coat the bluefish fillets with the mixture,
then lightly coat with a mixture of the
old Bay seasoning and the bread crumbs.
Bake in a 350-degree oven for 20
minutes or until fish is cooked.

SERVES 2.

From Fiddlers Sea Food Restaurant,
Chester, Connecticut

BROILED BLUEFISH BELLA VISTA

2 8-ounce bluefish fillets
6 strips bacon, sliced
1 small onion, julienned
1 green pepper, julienned
2 ripe tomatoes, peeled and diced
1/2 teaspoon chopped garlic
1/2 cup white wine
1 stick butter
1 lemon, cut in half

Sauté bacon. When half cooked, add onions, peppers, and tomatoes. Cook until onions and peppers are soft, then add garlic, 1/4 cup white wine, 1/2 stick butter, and juice from squeezed 1/2 lemon. Simmer 3 to 5 minutes.

Place bluefish in pan and top with 1/2

stick melted butter and 1/4 cup white
wine. Squeeze lemon half over fish.
Broil 8 to 10 minutes.

When done, top bluefish with sauce
and serve with rice.

          Serves 2

From the Mad Hatter Restaurant,
Nantucket.

Bluefish In Parchment

1½ lbs bluefish -
      Cut into 4 equal-size pieces, skinned & boned
2 carrots cut into matchsticks
2 celery stalks cut into matchsticks
1 TBS margarine   Thyme
Salt & pepper   Parchment Paper

Preheat oven to 400°

In a nonstick frying pan, Sauté the carrots and celery in the margarine until they are slightly cooked but still crunchy. Reheat frying pan over high heat. Quickly brown the fish pieces on both sides. Remove from heat.

Cut the parchment into 4 pieces about 17" wide, large enough to make a loose package when folded over the fish. Place a piece of fish in the center of each piece of parchment. Cover with some of the carrot and celery sticks. Sprinkle with thyme. Season to taste with salt and pepper.

Loosely wrap the fish and vegetables, folding the parchment over the fish and twisting the ends to close tightly. Place the pockets on an ungreased cookie sheet. Bake for 10 minutes. Serve each pocket on a dinner plate. Cut the parchment with a sharp knife or scissors and eat the fish directly from the parchment.

This is a low-calorie, delightful way to serve blues.

These pockets can be made up an hour or so before serving but should not be refrigerated.

Bluefish With Meringue

1 Fillet	1 Cup White Sauce (see recipe on page 43)
1 small onion, sliced	
1 tomato, peeled & sliced	3 egg whites
1 tsp chopped parsley	1/4 cup Parmesan Cheese
1/4 tsp thyme	
Salt & pepper	

Place fish in shallow baking dish. Broil for 10 minutes. Remove from broiler. Turn oven temperature to 350.°

Arrange slices of onion and tomato on top of the fish. Season with parsley and thyme. Add salt & pepper to taste. Pour white sauce over fish and vegetables. Whip egg whites until stiff. Spread over fish and sprinkle with cheese. Bake for 20 minutes or until meringue is brown.

A delight to the eye!

Blues In Crepes

<u>FRENCH</u>

1 Fillet, cooked and cut into 8 equal-size pieces
8 cooked crepes   2 TBS white wine
2 TBS butter or margarine   Salt & pepper
1 small onion, chopped   1 cup white sauce,
½ lb. mushrooms, sliced   see page 43
1 clove garlic, minced
1 small zucchini, grated and well drained

Preheat oven to 350°

In the butter sauté the onions, mushrooms and garlic, until limp over medium heat. Add zucchini and wine. Cover and simmer 3 minutes. Season to taste. Remove from heat. In the center of each crepe, place approximately 2 tablespoons of the vegetable mixture. Top this with a piece of fish. Fold the sides of the crepe over filling. Place in a baking dish. Cover with the sauce. Bake for 20 minutes.

ITALIAN

1 Fillet, cooked and cut into 8 equal-size pieces
8 cooked crepes
1 cup cottage cheese
2 scallions

1 tsp dill weed
salt & pepper
1 cup tomato sauce

Preheat oven to 350°.

Mix cottage cheese, scallions and dill. Season to taste. In the center of each crepe, place approximately 2 tablespoons of this mixture. Top with a piece of fish. Fold the sides of the crepe over the filling. Place in a baking dish. Cover with tomato sauce. Bake for 20 minutes.

↻ Crepes (10-12 crepes)

2 eggs, beaten
1/8 tsp salt
1 cup flour

1 cup milk
1 TBS melted butter or margarine

Combine eggs and salt. Alternately add the flour and milk. Beat until smooth. Add butter. Refrigerate for 2 hours. Cook in a 6-8" crepe pan or oiled frying pan.

New Orleans Blues- In Shells

1/2 lb Fillet - skinned and boned
4 large scallop shells (or small ramekins), greased
3 TBS margarine or butter
2 green onions
1 pkg frozen chopped creamed spinach - cooked
salt & pepper
4 slices crisp cooked bacon, crumbled
bread crumbs

Preheat oven to 375°.

Melt 1 TBS of the butter in a small pan. Sauté onions until limp. Add the spinach to the pan and stir. Season with salt and pepper. Cut bluefish into 4 equal portions, trying to keep the fish all the same thickness. Place each piece in the greased shells. Top with the bacon. Cover with the spinach/onion mixture. Sprinkle top of each with some bread crumbs. Dot with the remaining butter.

Place shells in a baking dish and bake
approximately 10 minutes or until a fork
pierces the fish easily.

Bluefish Rolls

1 or 2 fillets, depending on size of the fish
4 TBS butter - softened   flour
2 shallots - finely chopped   1 cup fine bread crumbs
½ tsp thyme   2 eggs
½ tsp dill   ½ cup milk
1 tsp parsley   oil for frying

Preheat oven to 350°.

Combine butter, shallots and herbs. Cut the fillet crosswise into 3" wide pieces. Spread a rounded teaspoonful of the butter-herb mixture on the fish slices. Roll up the slices and secure with a toothpick. Lightly flour the fish rolls. Beat eggs and milk together. Dip the rolls first into the egg mixture and then into the bread crumbs. Heat oil and brown the rolls on all sides. Place in an oven-proof dish and bake for 20 minutes.

Bluefish Pie

1 Fillet, skinned & boned
Pastry for 9" pie
4 oz. soft cream cheese
1/2 lb. mushrooms, sliced
1 small onion, chopped
1 TBS butter or margarine

1/2 head small cabbage, shredded
2 TBS white wine
1/2 tsp basil
1/2 tsp thyme
1/2 lb sausage meat

Preheat oven to 350°.
Roll out half the pastry for the bottom crust
and place in pie pan. Spread the cream
cheese over the bottom of the pastry. Set aside.
Cube the fish. Sauté mushrooms and onions in
butter until limp. Add shredded cabbage,
wine and herbs. Simmer 3 minutes. In another
pan, brown sausage meat, and then add fish.
Sauté several minutes until fish is cooked.
Drain excess grease. Combine fish and sausage

with vegetables. Place in crust over the
cream cheese. Cover with top crust.
Pierce top with fork to allow steam to
escape.
Bake in oven for 1 hour.

Blue Puffs

1 Fillet - cooked
2 sheets of puff pastry
1 pkg. frozen chopped spinach
feta Cheese
nutmeg

Preheat oven to 350°.

Cook spinach, then drain and squeeze out excess water. Divide the cooked fillet into eight equal pieces. Roll pastry sheets out and divide into four 5¼" squares. In the middle of each square place a rounded tablespoonful of spinach, a crumbling of feta cheese and a piece of bluefish. Sprinkle with nutmeg.

Fold the squares diagonally into triangles. Moisten edges with water and press to seal. Bake for 20 minutes or until puffed and browned.

Betsy's Blues

Moist and tender. Tastes like perfectly grilled fish.

1 ½ lbs. fillets
1 TBS margarine or butter

Place the butter* in a shallow baking dish in the oven and heat to 400° <u>without</u> the fish. When the oven has reached the temperature, place the fillets, skin side up, in the baking dish. Bake for 10 minutes. Turn** and bake 2-to 3 minutes more or until fish tests done. Serve with lemon wedges and/or tartar sauce.

* OR USE a nonstick spray
** At this point a lemon sauce, or any sauce of your choice, may be added if desired, but it is not necessary.

Black 'n' Blue fish

1 fillet
Cracked black peppercorns
1 tsp olive oil

Cut the fillet into 4 pieces. Press cracked pepper into fish. Place one piece of fish between two sheets of wax paper and flatten with a rolling pin. Repeat with the other pieces.

Heat a frying pan over medium-high heat. Add oil. Heat for a moment, then add the pieces of fish. Cook for 2 to 3 minutes on one side, turn, and cook 2 to 3 minutes on other side or until the fish flakes when tested with a fork.

This recipe is for hot (spicy) food lovers. Serve with fruit salad.

Bluefish Cutlets

1 Fillet	1 TBS butter or margarine
flour	1 TBS Capers
Salt & pepper	1 TBS White wine
1 TBS Olive oil	Worcestershire Sauce
½ lemon - sliced very thin	
Juice of ½ lemon	

Cut fillet into 4 equal pieces. Roll in flour
seasoned with salt & pepper. Place one piece
of fish between two sheets of wax paper
and flatten with a rolling pin down the
length of the fish. Repeat with the other pieces.
Heat a frying pan over medium-high heat.
Add olive oil. Heat for a few moments, then add
fish. Cook for 2 to 3 minutes on one side.
Turn and cook 2 to 3 minutes on the other side.
Transfer to a platter and keep warm. Add the

sliced lemon to the pan and sauté until the slices are limp. Add the butter, lemon juice, wine, worcestershire sauce and capers. Cook for a minute or two more. Pour sauce over fish cutlets and serve.

Even non-fish fanciers will fancy this one!

Vegetable Blue Sauté

1 Fillet
1 small eggplant, unpeeled - cubed
Olive Oil
1 small onion - Chopped   1 tsp basil
1/2 red pepper - diced   1 tsp parsley
1/2 green pepper - diced   1/4 tsp thyme
                                 1 large tomato - peeled
                                              and chopped

Sauté eggplant in 2 to 3 tbls. olive oil
over medium heat until it begins to
soften. Add onion, peppers, tomato, and
herbs (add more oil if needed). Sauté 2 to
3 minutes and add the cubed fish.
Continue to sauté until fish is cooked.
A lovely arrangement of colors.

Sauces

∿ <u>TOMATO - YOGURT</u>

2 cups yogurt
1 TBS finely minced onion
3 TBS TOMATO sauce
3 TBS KETCHUP
1/2 tsp sugar
1/2 tsp curry Powder
   SALT and PEPPER

mix all ingredients and refrigerate until
served.

∿ <u>SOUR CREAM AND DILL SAUCE</u>

1/2 cup sour CREAM or yogurt
   DILL - TO TASTE

mix sour CREAM and DILL and a pinch of SALT.

∿ GEOFF'S WHITE SAUCE FOR SMOKED FISH

2 TBS BUTTER	1 tsp DILL
1 TBS FLOUR	2 TBS VINEGAR
2 1/2 CUPS MILK	1 TBS HORSERADISH
1 tsp SALT	1/2 tsp GROUND GINGER
1 tsp PEPPER	1 TBS MAYONNAISE

MELT BUTTER UNTIL BUBBLING, STIR IN FLOUR and COOK FOR A FEW MINUTES. GRADUALLY ADD MILK, STIRRING UNTIL SAUCE IS SMOOTH and THICKENED. ADD REMAINING INGREDIENTS. SERVE OVER SMOKED BLUEFISH ON TOAST OR ON A MIXTURE OF FLAKED, SMOKED FISH and SCRAMBLED EGGS.

∾ HOLLANDAISE

3 EGG YOLKS
Juice of 1/2 lemon
1/4 tsp SALT
1/2 cup melted butter
  DASH OF PAPRIKA
  DASH OF CAYENNE PEPPER

PUT ALL INGREDIENTS, EXCEPT THE butter, INTO
A bLENDER AND mix bRIEFLY. MELT butter
UNTIL it bEGINS to bubble. GradUALLY ADD
butter to the blENDER while THE motor is
running. mix UNTIL smooth AND Thick.

～ SORREL SAUCE

¼ cup butter
¼ cup parmesan cheese
¼ cup olive oil
¼ cup pine nuts or small amount of peanuts
4 sprigs parsley
1 clove garlic
1 cup sorrel leaves

Combine all ingredients in blender and whirl until finely chopped. Serve at room temperature. Can be refrigerated, but allow to return to room temperature to serve.

∼ GREEN SAUCE

1 CLOVE GARLIC
4 TBS PARSLEY
2 ANCHOVIES
3 mushrooms
1 SMALL DILL PICKLE
1 SMALL SCALLION
1 SMALL STRIP OF GREEN or RED PEPPER
1 SMALL POTATO, PEELED and BOILED

2 tsp CAPERS
1 TBS PICKLE JUICE
1 TBS VINEGAR
1/2-3/4 CUP OLIVE OIL
1 EGG YOLK- HARD BOILED

FINELY CHOP and MASH TOGETHER ALL INGREDIENTS,
EXCEPT OIL, INTO A COARSE PASTE. FLOAT SOME
OIL ON TOP TO KEEP. PLACE IN A COOL SPOT,
UNREFRIGERATED AND COVERED. ADD MORE OIL AS
NECESSARY.

∿ ED'S <u>TOMATO SAUCE for BAKED BLUE</u>fish

2 CUPS TOMATO SAUCE
2 ONIONS - chopped
1 TBS Chopped DILL
1/2 tsp MINCED garLic
1/2 tsp freshly ground PEPPer
2 TBS OLIVE OiL
2 TBS VINEGar
1 TBS MiXED HErbs - oregANO, BASiL, ROSEMArY
1/2 CUP Sour CREAM
  PArSLEY
2 WhOLE fresh TOMATOES - QUArTErED

Simmer ALL iNgrediENTs, eXCEPT Sour CREAM, iN
coverEd Saucepan For 40 minuXes. Add the Sour
CREAM TO the Hot SauCE ANd Pour over HoT
BAKED BlueFish. GarNish with ParSLEY.

∿ MUSTARD - DILL SAUCE

1 CUP DIJON MUSTARD - 8 OZ JAR
1/3 CUP YOGURT or SOUR CREAM
1/3 CUP SUGAR
1/3 CUP WHITE VINEGAR
1 CUP OLIVE or VEG. OIL
1 CUP CHOPPED FRESH DILL
   SALT and PEPPER

MIX ALL INGREDIENTS EXCEPT OIL and DILL.
GRADUALLY STIR IN OIL UNTIL SMOOTH. THEN
STIR IN DILL. REFRIGERATE UNTIL SERVED.

∿ garLic MAYONNAisE

3 clOvEs garLic - 7iNELy chopped
2 EggS
6 TBS LEMON JuicE
1/2 tsp EAch SALT and PEpper
1 1/2 cup OLiVE OiL

BLENd ALL iNgREDIENTS, EXCEPT OiL, iN BLENDER.
THeN gradualLy pour iN oiL uNTiL THe mixture is
smooth ANd thickENED, But moRE Liquid thAN
reqular MAYONNAisE, AS you wish it as A
SAuce. COuER & REFRigErATE uNTiL SERuED.

    OR simply BLEND garLic with your 7Avorite
StorE - Bought MAYONNaisE.

~ BROWN BUTTER AND CAPERS

HEAT BUTTER UNTIL BROWNED. Add 2 tsp capers and 1 TBS LEMON JUICE. HEAT QUICKLY. POUR OVER FILLETS.

~ BUTTERS

ADD TO SOFTENED BUTTER ANY HERB - TARRAGON, ROSEMARY, CHIVES, PARSLEY, ETC. - TO YOUR TASTE.

Index to Recipes

Recipes for sauces begin on page 113.